C000225451

CLASSICAL FAVOURITES
Playalong *for* Clarinet

Wise Publications
part of The Music Sales Group
London/New York/Paris/Sydney/Copenhagen/Berlin/Madrid/Tokyo

Published by
Wise Publications
8/9 Frith Street, London W1D 3JB, UK.

Exclusive Distributors:
Music Sales Limited
Distribution Centre, Newmarket Road, Bury St. Edmunds,
Suffolk IP33 3YB, UK.
Music Sales Corporation
257 Park Avenue South, New York, NY10010, USA.
Music Sales Pty Limited
120 Rothschild Avenue, Rosebery, NSW 2018, Australia.

Order No. AM984456
ISBN 1-84609-307-4
This book © Copyright 2006 Wise Publications,
a division of Music Sales Limited.

Arranging and Engraving supplied by Camden Music.
Edited by Ann Farmer.
Cover photography by George Taylor.
Printed in Great Britain.

CDs recorded, mixed and mastered by Jonas Persson.
Instrumental solos by Jamie Talbot.
Piano: Tau Wey

www.musicsales.com

Clarinet Fingering Chart

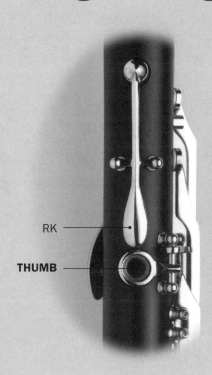

RK

THUMB

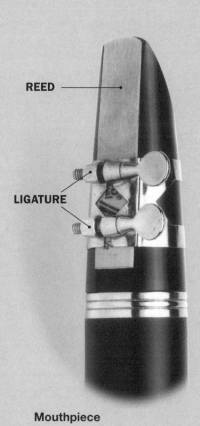

REED

LIGATURE

Mouthpiece

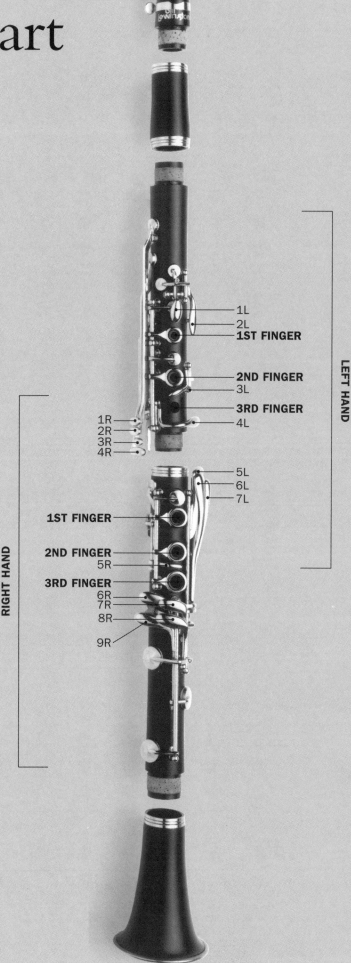

LEFT HAND

1L
2L
1ST FINGER
2ND FINGER
3L
3RD FINGER
4L

1R
2R
3R
4R

5L
6L
7L

RIGHT HAND

1ST FINGER
2ND FINGER
5R
3RD FINGER
6R
7R
8R
9R

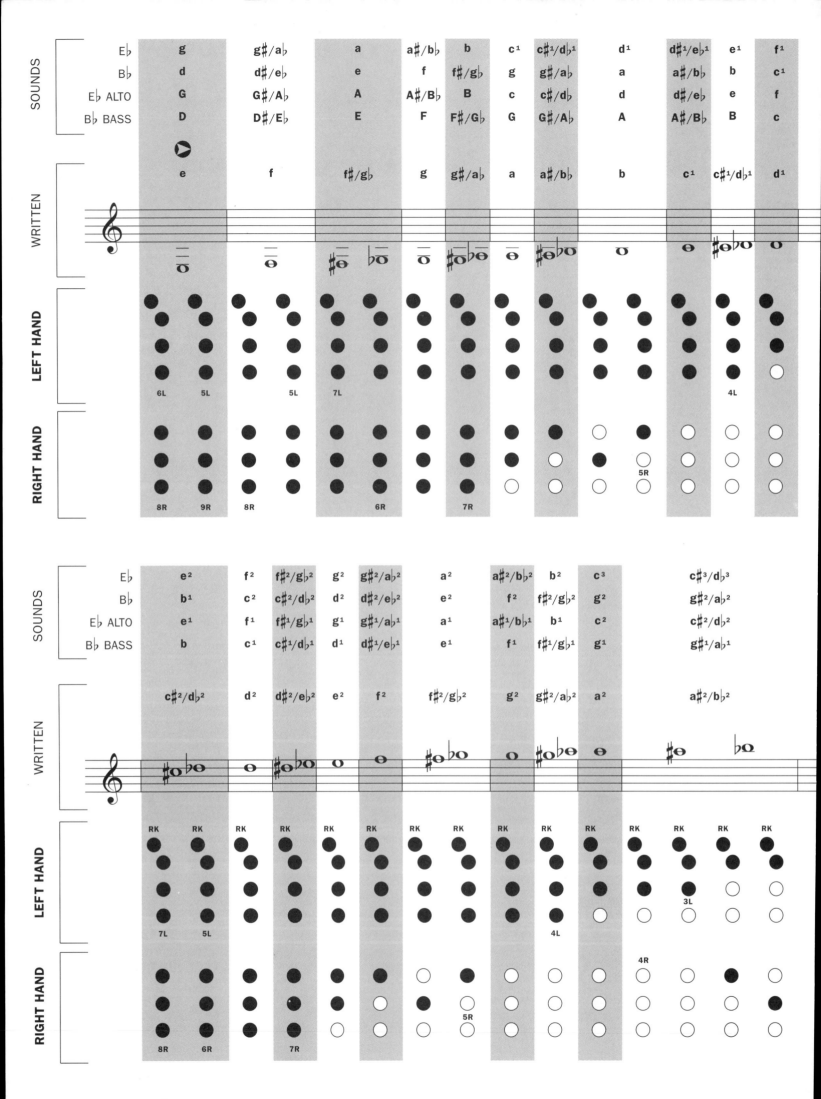

Indicates the lower limit of the best playing range for E♭, B♭, E♭ Alto and B♭ Bass Clarinets

Indicates the upper limit of the best playing range for E♭ and B♭ Clarinets

Indicates the upper limit of the best playing range for E♭ Alto and B♭ Bass Clarinets

A Musical Joke (Presto), K522

Composed by Wolfgang Amadeus Mozart

Air (from 'The Water Music')

Composed by George Frideric Handel

Moderato

Allegretto Theme (from Symphony No.7)

Composed by Ludwig van Beethoven

Allegretto ($\quarternote = 76$)

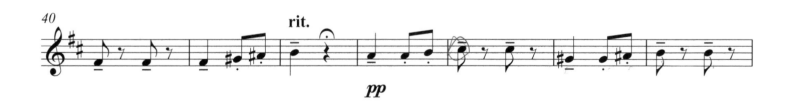

Ave Maria

Composed by Franz Peter Schubert

Entr'acte (from 'Rosamunde')

Composed by Franz Peter Schubert

Jerusalem

Composed by Hubert Parry

Jesu, Joy Of Man's Desiring

Composed by Johann Sebastian Bach

Largo (from 'Xerxes')

Composed by George Frideric Handel

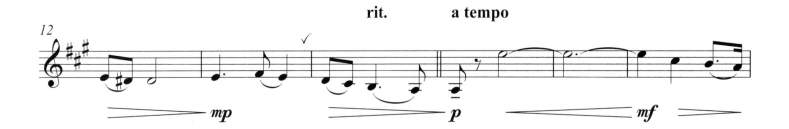

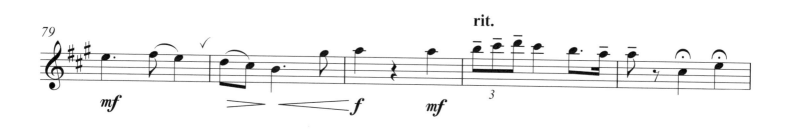

March (from 'The Nutcracker Suite')

Composed by Pyotr Ilyich Tchaikovsky

Tempo di marcia (♩ = 144)

O For The Wings Of A Dove

Composed by Felix Mendelssohn

Con moto (♩ = 69)

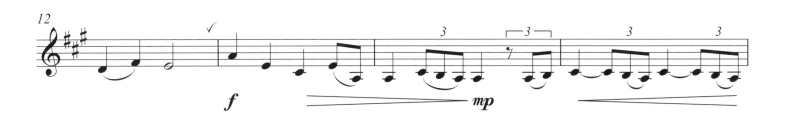

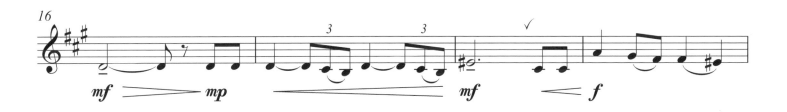

Sarabande (from Suite XI)

Composed by George Frideric Handel